THE RIGHT GAME

Harvard Business Review

CLASSICS

THE RIGHT GAME
*Use Game Theory to
Shape Strategy*

Adam M. Brandenburger
Barry J. Nalebuff

Harvard Business Press
Boston, Massachusetts

Library of Congress Cataloging-in-Publication Data
Brandenburger, Adam.
    The right game : use game theory to shape strategy / Adam M.
Brandenburger, Barry J. Nalebuff.
        p. cm. — (Harvard business review classics)
    "Reprint 95402"—T.p. verso.
    ISBN 978-1-63369-527-6
  1. Strategic planning. 2. Game theory. I. Nalebuff, Barry,
1958- II. Title.
    HD30.28.B6963 2009
    658.4'012—dc22
                                    2009021919

THE HARVARD BUSINESS
REVIEW CLASSICS SERIES

Since 1922, *Harvard Business Review* has
been a leading source of breakthrough ideas
in management practice—many of which still
speak to and influence us today. The HBR
Classics series now offers you the opportunity
to make these seminal pieces a part of your
permanent management library. Each volume
contains a groundbreaking idea that has
shaped best practices and inspired countless
managers around the world—and will change
how you think about the business world today.

THE RIGHT GAME

Business is a high-stakes game. The way we approach this game is reflected in the language we use to describe it. Business language is full of expressions borrowed from the military and from sports. Some of them are dangerously misleading. Unlike war and sports, business is not about winning and losing. Nor is it about how well you play the game. Companies can succeed spectacularly without requiring others to fail. And they can fail miserably no matter how well they play if they make the mistake of playing the wrong game.

The essence of business success lies in making sure you're playing the right game. How do you know if it's the right game? What can you do about it if it's the wrong game? To help managers answer those questions, we've developed a framework that draws on the insights of game theory. After 50 years as a mathematical construct, game theory is about to change the game of business.

Game theory came of age in 1994, when three pioneers in the field were awarded the Nobel Prize. It all began in 1944, when mathematics genius John von Neumann and economist Oskar Morgenstern published their book *Theory of Games and Economic Behavior*. Immediately heralded as one of the greatest scientific achievements of the century, their work provided a systematic way to understand the behavior of players in situations where their fortunes are interdependent. Von Neumann and Morgenstern distinguished two types of games. In the first type, rule-based games, players interact according to specified "rules of engagement." These rules might come from contracts, loan covenants, or trade agreements, for example. In the second type, freewheeling games, players interact without any external constraints. For example, buyers and sellers may create value by transacting in an unstructured fashion. Business is a complex mix of both types of games.

For rule-based games, game theory offers the principle, To every action, there is a reaction. But, unlike Newton's third law of motion, the reaction is not programmed to be equal and opposite. To analyze how other players will react to your move, you need to play out all the reactions (including yours) to their actions as far ahead as possible. You have to look forward far into the game and then reason backward to figure out which of today's actions will lead you to where you want to end up.[1]

For freewheeling games, game theory offers the principle, You cannot take away from the game more than you bring to it.

In business, what does a particular player
bring to the game? To find the answer, look
at the value created when everyone is in the
game, and then pluck that player out and see
how much value the remaining players can
create. The difference is the removed
player's "added value." In unstructured
interactions, you cannot take away more
than your added value.[2]

Underlying both principles is a shift
in perspective. Many people view games
egocentrically—that is, they focus on their
own position. The primary insight of game
theory is the importance of focusing on
others—namely, allocentrism. To look forward
and reason backward, you have to put yourself in the shoes—even in the heads—of other

players. To assess your added value, you have to ask not what other players can bring to you but what you can bring to other players.

Managers can profit by using these insights from game theory to design a game that is right for their companies. The rewards that can come from changing a game may be far greater than those from maintaining the status quo. For example, Nintendo succeeded brilliantly in changing the video game business by taking control of software. Sega's subsequent success required changing the game again. Rupert Murdoch's *New York Post* changed the tabloid game by finding a convincing way to demonstrate the cost of a price war without actually launching one. BellSouth made money by changing the

takeover game between Craig McCaw and
Lin Broadcasting. Successful business strategy is about actively shaping the game you
play, not just playing the game you find. We
will explore how these examples and others
worked in practice, starting with the story
of how General Motors changed the game
of selling cars.

FROM LOSE-LOSE TO WIN-WIN

In the early 1990s, the U.S. automobile
industry was locked into an all-too-familiar
mode of destructive competition. End-of-
year rebates and dealer discounts were ruin-
ing the industry's profitability. As soon as
one company used incentives to clear excess

inventory at year-end, others had to do the same. Worse still, consumers came to expect the rebates. As a result, they waited for them to be offered before buying a car, forcing manufacturers to offer incentives earlier in the year. Was there a way out? Would someone find an alternative to practices that were hurting all the companies? General Motors may have done just that.

In September 1992, General Motors and Household Bank issued a new credit card that allowed cardholders to apply 5% of their charges toward buying or leasing a new GM car, up to $500 per year, with a maximum of $3,500. The GM card has been the most successful credit-card launch in history. One month after it was introduced, there were

1.2 million accounts. Two years later, there were 8.7 million accounts—and the program is still growing. Projections suggest that eventually some 30% of GM's nonfleet sales in North America will be to cardholders.

As Hank Weed, managing director of GM's card program, explains, the card helps GM build share through the "conquest" of prospective Ford buyers and others—a traditional win-lose strategy. But the program has engineered another, more subtle change in the game of selling cars. It replaced other incentives that GM had previously offered. The net effect has been to raise the price that a noncardholder—someone who intends to buy a Ford, for example—would have to pay for a GM car. The program thus gives Ford some breathing room to raise its prices. That allows GM, in turn, to raise its prices without losing customers to Ford. The result is a win-win dynamic between GM and Ford.

If the GM card is as good as it sounds, what's stopping other companies from copying it? Not much, it seems. First, Ford introduced its version of the program with Citibank. Then Volkswagen introduced its variation with MBNA Corporation. Doesn't all this imitation put a dent in the GM program? Not necessarily. Imitation is the sincerest form of flattery, but in business it is often thought to be a killer compliment. Textbooks on strategy warn that if others can imitate something you do, you can't make money at it. Some go even further, asserting that business strategy cannot be codified. If it could, it would be imitated and any gains would evaporate.

Yet the proponents of this belief are mistaken in assuming that imitation is always harmful. It's true that once GM's program is widely imitated, the company's ability to lure customers away from other manufacturers will be diminished. But imitation also can help GM. Ford and Volkswagen offset the cost of their credit card rebates by scaling back other incentive programs. The result was an effective price increase for GM customers, the vast majority of whom do not participate in the Ford and Volkswagen credit card programs. This gives GM the option to firm up its demand or raise its prices further. All three car companies now have a more loyal customer base, so there is less incentive to compete on price.

To understand the full impact of the GM card program, you have to use game theory. You can't see all the ramifications of the program without adopting an allocentric perspective. The key is to anticipate how Ford, Volkswagen, and other auto-makers will respond to GM's initiative.

When you change the game, you want to come out ahead. That's pretty clear. But what about the fact that GM's strategy helped Ford? One common mind-set—seeing business as war—says that others have to lose in order for you to win. There may indeed be times when you want to opt for a win-lose strategy. But not always. The GM example shows that there also are times when you want to create a win-win situation. Although it may sound surprising, sometimes the best way to succeed is to let others, including your competitors, do well.

Looking for win-win strategies has several advantages. First, because the approach is relatively unexplored, there is greater potential for finding new opportunities. Second, because others are not being forced to give up ground, they may offer less resistance to win-win moves, making them easier to implement. Third, because win-win moves don't force other players to retaliate, the new game is more sustainable. And finally, imitation of a win-win move is beneficial, not harmful.

To encourage thinking about both cooperative and competitive ways to change the game, we suggest the term *coopetition*.[3] It means looking for win-win as well as win-lose opportunities. Keeping both possibilities in mind is important because win-lose strategies often backfire. Consider, for example, the common—and dangerous—strategy of lowering prices to gain market share. Although it may provide a temporary benefit, the gains will evaporate if others match the cuts to regain their lost share. The result is simply to reestablish the status quo but at lower prices—a lose-lose scenario that leaves all the players worse off. That was the situation in the automobile industry before GM changed the game.

THE GAME OF BUSINESS

Did GM intentionally plan to change the game of selling cars in the way we have described it? Or did the company just get lucky with a loyalty marketing program that turned out better than anyone had expected? Looking back, the one thing we can say with certainty is that the stakes in situations like GM's are too high to be left to chance. That's why we have developed a comprehensive map and a method to help managers find strategies for changing the game.

The game of business is all about value: creating it and capturing it. Who are the participants in this enterprise? To describe them, we introduce the Value Net—a schematic map designed to represent all the players in the game and the interdependencies among them. (See the exhibit "Who Are the Players in Your Company's Value Net?")

Interactions take place along two dimensions. Along the vertical dimension are the company's customers and suppliers.

Who are the players in your company's value net?

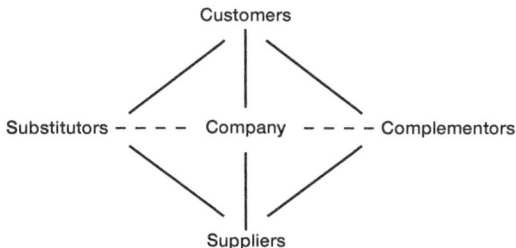

Resources such as labor and raw materials flow from the suppliers to the company, and products and services flow from the company to its customers. Money flows in the reverse direction, from customers to the company and from the company to its suppliers. Along the horizontal dimension are the players with whom the company interacts but does not transact. They are its *substitutors* and *complementors*.

Substitutors are alternative players from whom customers may purchase products or to whom suppliers may sell their resources. Coca-Cola and Pepsico are substitutors with respect to consumers because they sell rival colas. A little less obvious is that Coca-Cola and Tyson Foods are substitutors with respect to suppliers. That is because both companies use carbon dioxide. Tyson uses it for freezing chickens, and Coke uses it for carbonation. (As they say in the cola industry, "No fizziness, no bizziness.")

Complementors are players from whom customers buy complementary products or to whom suppliers sell complementary resources. For example, hardware and software companies are classic complementors. Faster hardware, such as a Pentium chip, increases users' willingness to pay for more powerful software. More powerful software, such as the latest version of Microsoft Office, increases users' willingness to pay for faster hardware. American Airlines and United Air Lines, though substitutors with respect to passengers, are complementors when they decide to update their fleets. That's because Boeing can recoup the cost of a new plane design only if enough airlines buy it. Since each airline effectively subsidizes the other's purchase of planes, the two are complementors in this instance.

We introduce the terms *substitutor* and *complementor* because we find that the traditional business vocabulary inhibits a full understanding of the interdependencies that exist in business. If you call a player a competitor, you tend to focus on competing rather than on finding opportunities for co-operation. *Substitutor* describes the market relationship without that prejudice. Complementors, often overlooked in traditional strategic analysis, are the natural counter-parts of substitutors.

The Value Net describes the various roles of the players. It's possible for the same player to occupy more than one role simultaneously. Remember that American and United are both substitutors and complementors. Gary Hamel and C.K. Prahalad make this point in *Competing for the Future* (Harvard Business School Press, 1994): "On any given day . . . AT&T might find Motorola to be a supplier, a buyer, a competitor, *and* a partner."

The Value Net reveals two fundamental symmetries in the game of business: the first between customers and suppliers and the second between substitutors and complementors. Understanding those symmetries can help managers come up with new strategies for changing the game or new applications of existing strategies.

Managers understand intuitively that along the vertical dimension of the Value Net, there is a mixture of cooperation and competition. It's cooperation when suppliers, companies, and customers come together to create value in the first place. It's competition when the time comes for them to divide the pie.

Along the horizontal dimension, however, managers tend to see only half the picture. Substitutors are seen only as enemies. Complementors, if viewed at all, are seen only as friends. Such a perspective overlooks another symmetry. There can be a cooperative element to interactions with substitutors, as the GM story illustrates, and a competitive element to interactions with complementors, as we will see.

CHANGING THE GAME

The Value Net is a map that prompts you to explore all the interdependencies in the game. Drawing the Value Net for your business is therefore the first step toward changing the game. The second step is identifying all the elements of the game. According to game theory, there are five: players, added values, rules, tactics, and scope—PARTS for short. These five elements fully describe all interactions, both freewheeling and rule-based. To change the game, you have to change one or more of these elements.

Players come first. As we saw in the Value Net, the players are customers, suppliers, substitutors, and complementors. None of the players are fixed. Sometimes it's smart to change who is playing the game. That includes yourself.

Added values are what each player brings to the game. There are ways to make yourself a more valuable player–in other words, to raise your added value. And there are ways to lower the added values of other players.

Rules give structure to the game. In business, there is no universal set of rules; a rule might arise from law, custom, practicality, or contracts. In addition to using existing rules to their advantage, players may be able to revise them or come up with new ones.

Scope describes the boundaries of the game. It's possible for players to expand or shrink those boundaries.

Successful business strategies begin by assessing and then changing one or more of these elements. PARTS does more than exhort you to think out of the box. It provides the tools to enable you to do so. Let's look at each strategic lever in turn.

CHANGING THE PLAYERS

NutraSweet, a low-calorie sweetener used in soft drinks such as Diet Coke and Diet Pepsi, is a household name, and its swirl logo is recognized worldwide. In fact, it's Monsanto's brand name for the chemical aspartame. NutraSweet has been a very profitable business for Monsanto, with 70% gross margins. Such profits usually attract others to enter the market, but NutraSweet was protected by patents in Europe until 1987 and in the United States until 1992.

With Coke's blessing, a challenger, the Holland Sweetener Company, built an aspartame plant in Europe in 1985 in anticipation of the patent expiration. Ken Dooley, HSC's vice president of marketing and sales, explained, "Every manufacturer likes to have at least two sources of supply."

As HSC attacked the European market, Monsanto fought back aggressively. It used deep price cuts and contractual relationships with customers to deny HSC a toehold in the market. HSC managed to fend off the initial counterattack by appealing to the courts to enable it to gain access to customers. Dooley considered all this just a preview of things to come: "We are looking forward to moving the war into the United States."

But Dooley's war ended before it began. Just prior to the U.S. patent expiration, both Coke and Pepsi signed new long-term contracts with Monsanto. When at last there was a real potential for competition between suppliers, it appeared that Coke and Pepsi didn't seize the opportunity. Or did they?

Neither Coke nor Pepsi ever had any real desire to switch over to generic aspartame. Remembering the result of the New Coke

reformulation of 1985, neither company
wanted to be the first to take the NutraSweet
logo off the can and create a perception that
it was fooling around with the flavor of its
drinks. If only one switched over, the other
most certainly would have made a selling
point of its exclusive use of NutraSweet.
After all, NutraSweet had already built
a reputation for safety and good taste. Even
though generic aspartame would taste the
same, consumers would be unfamiliar with
the unbranded product and see it as inferior.
Another reason not to switch was that Monsanto had spent the previous decade march-
ing down the learning curve for making
aspartame–giving it a significant cost
advantage–while HSC was still near the top.

In the end, what Coke and Pepsi really wanted was to get the same old NutraSweet at a much better price. That they accomplished. Look at Monsanto's position before and after HSC entered the game. Before, there was no good substitute for NutraSweet. Cyclamates had been banned, and saccharin caused cancer in laboratory rats. NutraSweet's added value was its ability to make a safe, good-tasting low-calorie drink possible. Stir in a patent and things looked very positive for Monsanto. When HSC came along, NutraSweet's added value was greatly reduced. What was left was its brand loyalty and its manufacturing cost advantage.

Where did all this leave HSC? Clearly, its entry into the market was worth a lot to

Coke and Pepsi. It would have been quite reasonable for HSC, before entering the market, to demand compensation for its role in the form of either a fixed payment or a guaranteed contract. But, once in, with an unbranded product and higher production costs, it was much more difficult for the company to make money. Dooley was right when he said that all manufacturers want a second source. The problem is, they don't necessarily want to do much business with that source.

Monsanto did well to create a brand identity and a cost advantage: It minimized the negative effects of entry by a generic brand. Coke and Pepsi did well to change the game by encouraging the entry of a new player that would reduce their dependence on NutraSweet. According to HSC, the new contracts led to combined savings of $200 million annually for Coke and Pepsi. As for HSC, perhaps it was too quick to become a player. The question for HSC was not what it could do for Coke and Pepsi; the question was what Coke and Pepsi could do for HSC. Although it was a duopolist in a weak position when it came to selling aspartame, HSC was a monopolist in a strong position when it came to selling its "service" to make the aspartame market competitive. Perhaps Coke and Pepsi would have paid a higher price for this valuable service, but only if HSC had demanded such payment up front.

Pay Me to Play

As the NutraSweet story illustrates, sometimes the most valuable service you can offer
is creating competition, so don't give it away
for free. People in the takeover game have
long understood the art of getting paid to
play. The cellular phone business was under-
going rapid consolidation in June 1989,
when 39-year-old Craig Mc-Caw made a bid
for Lin Broadcasting Corporation. With
50 million POPs (lingo for the population
in a coverage area) already under his belt,
McCaw saw the acquisition of Lin's 18 million POPs as the best, and possibly the only,
way to acquire a national cellular footprint.
He bid $120 per share for Lin, which

resulted in an immediate jump in Lin's share price from $103.50 to $129.50. Clearly, the market expected more action. But Lin's CEO, Donald Pels, didn't care much for McCaw or his bid. Faced with Lin's hostile reaction, McCaw lowered his offer to $110, and Lin sought other suitors. BellSouth, with 28 million POPs, was the natural alternative, although acquiring Lin wouldn't quite give it a national footprint.

Nevertheless, BellSouth was willing to acquire Lin for the right price. But if it entered the fray, it would create a bidding war and thus make it unlikely that Lin would be sold for a reasonable price. BellSouth knew that only one bidder could win, and it wanted something in case that bidder was McCaw.

Thus, as a condition for making a bid, BellSouth got Lin's promise of a $54 million consolation prize and an additional $15 million toward expenses in the event that it was outbid. BellSouth made an offer generally valued at between $105 and $112 per share. As expected, BellSouth was outbid; McCaw responded with an offer valued at $112 to $118 per share. BellSouth then raised its bid to roughly $120 per share. In return, Lin raised BellSouth's expense cap to $25 million. McCaw raised his bid to $130 and then added a few dollars more to close the deal. At the same time, he paid BellSouth $22.5 million to exit the game.[4] At this point in the bidding, Lin's CEO recognized that his stock options were worth $186 million, and the now friendly deal with McCaw was concluded.

So how did the various players make out? Lin got itself an extra billion, which made its $79 million payment to BellSouth look like a bargain. McCaw got the national network he wanted and subsequently sold out to AT&T, making himself a billionaire. And BellSouth, by getting paid first to play and then to go away, turned a weak hand into $76.5 million plus expenses.

BellSouth clearly understood that even if you can't make money in the game the old-fashioned way, you can get paid to change it. Such payments need not be made in cash; you can ask for a guaranteed sales contract, contributions to R&D, bid-preparation expenses, or a last-look provision.

The examples so far show how you can change three of the four players in the Value Net. Lin paid to bring in an extra buyer, or customer. Coke and Pepsi would, no doubt, have been prepared to pay HSC handsomely to become a second supplier. And McCaw paid to take out a rival bidder, or substitutor. That leaves complementors. The next example shows how a company can benefit from bringing players into the complements market.

Cheap Complements

Remember that hardware is the classic complement to software. One can't function without the other. Software writers won't produce programs unless a sufficient hardware base exists. Yet consumers won't purchase the hardware until a critical mass of software exists. 3DO Company, a maker of video games, is attacking this chicken-and-egg problem in the video-game business by bringing players into the complements market. To those who know 3DO's founder, Trip Hawkins, this should come as no surprise: He designed his own major at Harvard in strategy and game theory.

3DO owns a 32-bit CD-ROM hardware-and-software technology for next-generation video games. The company plans to make money by licensing software houses to make 3DO games and collecting a $3 royalty fee (hence the company name). Of course, to sell software, you first need people to buy the hardware. But those early adopters won't find much software. To start the ball rolling, 3DO needs the hardware to be cheap—the cheaper the better.

The company's strategy is to give away the license to produce the hardware technology. This move has induced hardware manufacturers such as Panasonic (Matsushita), GoldStar, Sanyo, and Toshiba to enter the game. Because all 3DO software will run on all 3DO hardware, the hardware manufacturers are left to compete on cost alone. Making the hardware a commodity is just what 3DO wants: It drives down the price of the complementary product.

But not quite enough. 3DO is discovering that to create momentum in the market, the hardware must be sold below cost, and hardware manufacturers aren't willing to go that far. As an inducement, 3DO now offers them two shares of 3DO stock for each machine sold. The company also has renegotiated its deal with software houses up to a $6 royalty, with the extra $3 earmarked to subsidize hardware sales. So Hawkins is actually paying people to play in the complements market. Is he paying enough? Time will tell.

Creating competition in the complements market is the flip side of coopetition. Just as substitutors are usually seen only as enemies, complementors are seen only as friends. Whereas the GM story shows the possibility of win-win opportunities with substitutors, the 3DO example illustrates the possibility of legitimate win-lose opportunities with complementors. Creating competition among its complementors helped 3DO at their expense.

CHANGING THE ADDED VALUES

Just as you shouldn't accept the players of a game as fixed, you shouldn't take what they bring to the game as fixed, either. You can change the players' added values. Common sense tells us that there are two options: Raise your own added value or lower that of others.

Good basic business practices are one route to raising added values. You can tailor your product to customers' needs, build a brand, use resources more efficiently, work

with your suppliers to lower their costs, and
so on. These strategies should not be under-
estimated. But there are other, less transpar-
ent ways to raise your added value. As an
example, consider Trans World Airlines'
introduction of Comfort Class in 1993.

Robert Cozzi, TWA's senior vice president of marketing, proposed removing 5 to
40 seats per plane to give passengers in
coach more legroom. The move raised
TWA's added value; according to J.D. Power
and Associates, the company soared to first
place in customer satisfaction for long-haul
flights. This was a win for TWA and a loss for
other airlines. But elements of win-win were
present as well: With fuller planes, TWA was
not about to start a price war.

But what if other carriers copied the strategy? Would that negate TWA's efforts? No, because as others copied TWA's move, excess capacity would be retired from an industry plagued by overcapacity. Passengers get more legroom, and carriers stop flying empty seats around. Everyone wins. Cozzi saw a way to move the industry away from the self-defeating price competition that goes on when airlines try to fill up the coach cabin. This was business strategy at its best.[5]

The idea of raising your own added value is natural. Less intuitive is the approach of lowering the added value of others. To illustrate how the strategy works, let's begin with a simple card game.

Adam M. Brandenburger and Barry J. Nalebuff

Adam and 26 of his M.B.A. students are playing a card game. Adam has 26 black cards, and each of the students has one red card. Any red card coupled with a black card gets a $100 prize (paid by the dean). How do we expect the bargaining between Adam and his students to proceed?

First, calculate the added values. Without Adam and his black cards, there is no game. Thus Adam's added value equals the total value of the game, which is $2,600. Each student has an added value of $100 because without that student's card, one less match can be made and thus $100 is lost. The sum of the added values is therefore $5,200—made up of $2,600 from Adam and $100 from each of the 26 students. Alas, there is only $2,600 to be divided. Given the symmetry of the game, it's most likely that everyone will end up with half of his or her added value: Adam will buy the students' cards for $50 each or sell his for $50 each.

So far, nothing is surprising. Could Adam do any better? Yes, but first he'd have to change the game.

In a public display, Adam burns three of his black cards. True, the pie is now smaller, at $2,300, and so is Adam's added value. But the point of this strategic move is to destroy the added values of the other players. Now no student has any added value because 3 students are going to end up without a match, and therefore no one student is essential to the game. The total value with 26 students is $2,300, and the total value with 25 students is still $2,300.

At this point, the division will not be equal. Indeed, because no student has any added value, Adam would be quite generous to offer a 90:10 split. Since 3 students will end up with nothing, anyone who ends up with $10 should consider himself or herself lucky. For Adam, 90% of $2,300 is a lot better than half of $2,600. Of course, his getting it depends on the students' not being able to get together; if they did, that would be changing the game, too. In fact, it would be changing the players, as in the previous section, and it would be an excellent strategy for the students to adopt.

Just a card trick? No—a strategy employed by the video-game maker Nintendo (which, it so happens, used to produce playing cards). To see how the company lowered everyone else's added value, we take a tour around its Value Net. (See the exhibit "Nintendo Trumped Every Player in Its Value Net.")

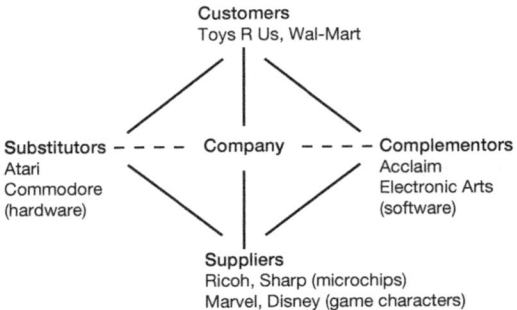

Nintendo trumped every player in its value net

```
                        Customers
                        Toys R Us, Wal-Mart
                          /        \
                         /          \
Substitutors  – – –  Company  – – –  Complementors
Atari                  \          /   Acclaim
Commodore               \        /    Electronic Arts
(hardware)               \      /     (software)
                        Suppliers
                        Ricoh, Sharp (microchips)
                        Marvel, Disney (game characters)
```

Nintendo Power

Start with Nintendo's customers. Nintendo sold its games to a highly concentrated market—predominantly megaretailers such as Toys R Us and Wal-Mart. How could Nintendo combat such buyer power? By changing the game. Nintendo did just what Adam did when he burned the cards (although Nintendo made a lot more money): It didn't fill all the retailers' orders. In 1988, Nintendo sold 33 million cartridges, but the market could have absorbed 45 million. Poor planning? No. It's true that the pie shrank a little as some stores sold out of the game. But the important point is that retailers lost added value. Even a giant like Toys R Us was in a weaker position when not every retailer could get supplied. As Nintendomania took hold, consumers queued up outside stores and retailers clamored for more of the product. With games in short supply, Nintendo had zapped the buyers' power.

The next arena of negotiations concerned the complementors—namely, outside game developers. What was Nintendo's strategy? First, it developed software in-house. The company built a security chip into the hardware and then instituted a licensing program for outside developers. The number of licenses was restricted, and licensees were allowed to develop only a limited number of games. Because there were many Nintendo wanna-be programmers and because the company could develop games inhouse, the added value of those that did get the license was lowered. Once again, Nintendo ensured that there were fewer black cards than red. It held all the bargaining chips.

Nintendo's suppliers, too, had little added value. The company used old-generation chip technology, making its chips something of a commodity. Another input was the leading characters in the games. Nintendo hit the jackpot by developing Mario. After he became a hit in his own right, the added value of comic-book heroes licensed from others, such as Spiderman (Marvel), and of cartoon icons, such as Mickey Mouse (Disney), was reduced. In fact, Nintendo turned the tables completely, licensing Mario to appear in comic books and on cartoon shows, cereal boxes, board games, and toys.

Finally, there were Nintendo's substitutors. From a kid's perspective, there were no good alternatives to a video game; the only real threat came from alternative video-game systems. Here Nintendo had the game practically all to itself. Having the largest installed base of systems allowed the company to drive down the manufacturing cost for its hardware. And with developers keen to write for the largest installed base, Nintendo got the best games. This created a positive feedback loop: More people bought Nintendo's systems, leading to a larger base, still lower costs, and even more games. Nintendo locked in its lead by requiring exclusivity from outside game developers. With few alternatives to Nintendo, that was a small price for them to pay. Potential challengers couldn't simply take successful games over to their platforms; they had to start from scratch. Although large profits might normally invite entry, no challenger could engineer any added value. The installed base, combined with Nintendo's exclusivity agreements, made competing in Nintendo's game hopeless.

What was the bottom line for Nintendo? How much could a manufacturer of a two-bit—well, eight-bit—game about a lugubrious plumber called Mario really be worth? How about more than Sony or Nissan? Between July 1990 and June 1991, Nintendo's average market value was

2.4 trillion yen, Sony's was 2.2 trillion yen, and Nissan's was 2 trillion yen.

The Nintendo example illustrates the importance of added value as opposed to value. There is no doubt that cars, televisions, and VCRs create more value in the world than do Game Boys. But it's not enough simply to create value; profits come from capturing value. By keeping its added value high and everyone else's low, Nintendo was able to capture a giant slice of a largish pie. The name of the enthusiasts' monthly magazine, *Nintendo Power*, summed up the situation quite nicely.

Nintendo's success, however, brought it under scrutiny. In late 1989, Congressman Dennis Eckart (D-Ohio), chairman of the House Subcommittee on Antitrust, Impact of Deregulation and Privatization, requested that the U.S. Justice Department investigate allegations that Nintendo of America unfairly reduced competition. Eckart's letter argued, among other things, that the Christmas shortages in 1988 were "contrived to increase consumer prices and demand and to enhance Nintendo's market leverage" and that software producers had "become almost entirely dependent on Nintendo's acceptance of their games." None of Nintendo's practices were found to be illegal.[6]

Pumping Up Profits

Protecting your added value is as important as establishing it in the first place. Back in the mid-1970s, Robert Taylor, CEO of

Minnetonka, had the idea for Softsoap, a
liquid soap that would be dispensed by a
pump. The problem was that it would be hard
to retain any added value once the likes of
Procter & Gamble and Lever Brothers mus-
cled in with their brands and distribution
clout. Nothing in the product could be
patented. But, to his credit, Taylor realized
that the hardest part of producing the soap
was manufacturing the little plastic pump,
for which there were just two suppliers. In a
bet-the-company move, he locked up both
suppliers' total annual production by order-
ing 100 million of the pumps. Even at 12
cents apiece, this was a $12 million order—
more than Minnetonka's net worth. Ulti-
mately, the major players did enter the market,

but capturing the supply of pumps gave Taylor a head start of 12 to 18 months. That advantage preserved Softsoap's added value during this period, allowing the company to build brand loyalty, which continues to provide added value to this day.

As the TWA, Nintendo, and Softsoap examples illustrate, added values can be changed. By reengineering them—raising your added value and lowering others'—you may be able to capture a larger slice of pie.

Game theory holds that in freewheeling interactions, no player can take away more than that player brings to the game, but that's not quite the end of the matter. First, there is no guarantee that any player will get all its added value. Typically, the sum of all the added values exceeds the total value of the game. Remember that in Adam's card game, the total prize was only $2,600 even though the added values of all the players initially totaled $5,200. Second, even if you have no added value, that doesn't prohibit you from making money. Others might be willing to pay you to enter or exit the game (as with BellSouth); similarly, you might be paid to stay out or stay in. Third, rules constrain interactions among players. We will see that in games with rules, some players may be able to capture more than their added values.

CHANGING THE RULES

Rules determine how the game is played by limiting the possible reactions to any action.

To analyze the effect of a rule, you have to look forward and reason backward.

The simplest rule is *one price to all*. According to this rule, prices are not negotiated individually with each customer. Consequently, a company can profitably enter a market even when it has no added value. If a new player enters with a price lower than the incumbent's, the incumbent has only two effective responses: match the newcomer's price across the board or stand pat and give up share. By looking forward and reasoning backward, a small newcomer can steer the incumbent toward accommodation rather than retaliation.

Imagine that a new player comes in with a limited capacity—say, 10% of the market—and a discounted price. Whether it makes any money depends on how the incumbent responds. The incumbent can recapture its lost market by coming down to match the newcomer's price, or it can give up 10% share. For the incumbent, giving up 10% share is usually better than sacrificing its profit margin. In such cases, the newcomer will do all right. But it can't get too greedy. If it tries to take away too much of the market, the incumbent will choose to give up its profit margin in order to regain share. Only when the newcomer limits its capacity does the incumbent stand pat and the newcomer make money. For this reason, the strategy is called *judo economics:* By staying small, the newcomer turns the incumbent's larger size to its own benefit.

To pull off a judo strategy, the newcomer's commitment to limit its capacity must be both clear and credible. The newcomer may be tempted to expand, but it must realize that if it does, it will give the incumbent an incentive to retaliate.

Kiwi Is No Dodo

Kiwi International Air Lines understands these ideas perfectly. Named for the flightless bird, Kiwi is a 1992 start-up founded by former Eastern Air Lines pilots who were grounded after Eastern went bankrupt. Kiwi engineered a cost advantage from its employee ownership and its use of leased planes. But it had lower name recognition and a more limited flight schedule than the major carriers—on balance, not much, if any, added value. So what did it do? It went for low prices and limited capacity. According to public statements from its then CEO, Robert Iverson, "We designed our system to stay out of the way of large carriers and to make sure they understand that we pose no threat. . . . Kiwi intends to capture, at most, only 10% share of any one market—or no more than four flights per day." Because Kiwi targets business travelers, the major airlines can't use stay-over and advance-purchase restrictions to lower price selectively against it. So Kiwi benefited from the one-price-to-all rule.

Now Kiwi, in turn, became the large player for any newcomer to the same market.

That didn't leave much room to be small in relation to Kiwi, so Kiwi had to fight if someone else tried to follow suit. According to Iverson, "[The major airlines] are better off with us than without us." Even though Kiwi was Delta's rival, by staying small and keeping out other potential entrants, it managed to bring an element of coopetition into the game. From Delta's perspective, Kiwi was rather like the devil it knew.

The Kiwi story illustrates how a player can take advantage of existing rules of the marketplace—in this case, the one-price-to-all rule. In addition to practicality, rules arise from custom, law, or contracts. Common contract-based rules are mostfavored-nation (most-favored-customer) clauses, take-or-pay agreements, and meet-the-competition clauses. These rules give structure to negotiations between buyers and sellers. Rules are particularly useful for players in commodity-like businesses. As an example, take the carbon dioxide industry.

Solid Profits from Gas

There are three major producers of carbon dioxide: Airco, Liquid Carbonic, and Air Liquide. Carbon dioxide creates enormous value (in carbonation and freezing), but it is essentially a commodity, which makes it hard for a producer to capture any of that value. One distinguishing factor, however, is that carbon dioxide is very expensive to transport, which gives some added value to the producer best located to serve a specific customer. Other sources of added value are differentiation through reliability, reputation, service, and technology. Still, a producer's added value is usually small in relation to the total value created. The question is, Can a producer capture more than its added value?

In this case the answer is yes, because of the rules of the game in the carbon dioxide industry. The producers have a meet-the-competition clause (MCC) in their contracts with customers. An MCC gives the incumbent seller the right to make the last bid.

The result of an MCC is that a producer can sustain a higher price and thereby earn more than its added value. Normally, an elevated price would invite other producers to compete on price. In this case, however, a challenger cannot come in and take away business simply by undercutting the existing price. If it tried, the incumbent could then come back with a lower price and keep the business. The back-and-forth could go on until the price fell to variable cost, but at that point stealing the business wouldn't be worth the effort. The only one to benefit would be the buyer, who would end up with a lower price.

Cutting price to go after an incumbent's business is always risky but may be justified by the gain in business. Not so when the incumbent has an MCC: The upside is lost and the downside remains. Lowering price sets a dangerous precedent and increases the

likelihood of a tit-for-tat response. The
incumbent may retaliate by going after the
challenger's business, and even if the challenger doesn't lose customers, it certainly
will lose profits. Another downside is that
the challenger's customers may end up at a
disadvantage. If the challenger supplies
Coke and the incumbent supplies Pepsi,
the challenger shouldn't help Pepsi get a
lower price. Its future is tied to Coke, and
it doesn't want to give Pepsi any cost
advantage. It might even end up having to
lower its own price to Coke without getting
Pepsi's business. Finally, the challenger's
efforts are misplaced: It would do better
to make sure that its existing customers
are happy.

Putting in an MCC changes the game in a way that's clearly a win for the incumbent. Perhaps surprisingly, the challenger also ends up better off. True, it may not be able to take away market share, but the incumbent's higher prices set a good precedent: They give the challenger some room to raise prices to its own customers. There also is less danger that the incumbent will go after the challenger's share, because the incumbent, with higher profits, now has more to lose. An MCC is a classic case of coopetition.

As for the customers, why do they go along with this rule? It may be traditional in their industry. Perhaps it's the norm. Perhaps they decide to trade an initial price break in return for the subsequent lock-in.

Or maybe they don't thoroughly understand the rule's implications. Whatever the reason, MCCs do offer benefits to customers. The clauses guarantee producers a long-term relationship if they so choose, even in the absence of long-term contracts. Thus producers are more willing to invest in serving their customers. Finally, even if there is no formal MCC, it's generally accepted that you don't leave your current supplier without giving it a last chance to bid.

Using an MCC is a strategy that, far from being undermined by imitation, is enhanced by it. A carbon dioxide producer benefits from unilateral adoption of an MCC, but there is an added kicker when other producers copy it. The MCCs allow them to push prices up

further, so they now have even more to lose
from starting a share war. As MCCs become
more widespread, everyone has less prospect
of gaining share. With even more at risk and
even less to gain, producers refrain from
going after one another's customers. A moral:
Players who live in glass houses are unlikely to
throw stones. So you should be pleased when
others build glass houses.

Both the significance of rules and the
opportunity to change the game by changing
the rules are often underappreciated. If
negotiations in your business take place without rules, consider how bringing in a new
rule would change the game. But be careful.
Just as you can rewrite rules and make new
ones, so, too, can others. Unlike other

games, business has no ultimate rule-making authority to settle disputes. History matters. The government can make some rules–through antitrust laws, for example. In the end, however, the power to make rules comes largely from power in the market-place. While it's true that rules can trump added value, it is added value that confers the power to make rules in the first place. As they said in the old West, "A Smith & Wesson beats a straight flush."

TACTICS: CHANGING PERCEPTIONS

We've changed the players, their added values, and the rules. Is there anything left to change? Yes–perceptions. There is no guarantee that everyone agrees on who the players are, what their added values are, and what the rules are. Nor are the implications of every move and countermove likely to be clear. Business is mired in uncertainty. Tactics influence the way players perceive the uncertainty and thus mold their behavior. Some tactics work by reducing misperceptions—in other words, by lifting the fog. Others work by creating or maintaining uncertainty—by thickening the fog.

Here we offer two examples. The first shows how Rupert Murdoch lifted the fog to influence how the *New York Daily News* perceived the game; the second illustrates how maintaining a fog can help negotiating parties reach an agreement.

The New York Fog

In the beginning of July 1994, the *Daily News* raised its price from 40 cents to 50 cents. This seemed rather remarkable under the circumstances. Its major rival, Rupert Murdoch's *New York Post*, was test-marketing a price cut to 25 cents and had demonstrated its effectiveness on Staten Island. As the *New York Times* saw it (Press Notes, July 4), it was as if the *Daily News* were daring Murdoch to follow through with his price cut. But, in fact, there was more going on than the *Times* realized. Murdoch had earlier raised the price of the *Post* to 50 cents, and the *Daily News* had held at 40 cents. As a result, the *Post* was losing subscribers and, with them, advertising revenue. Whereas Murdoch viewed the situation as unsustainable, the *Daily News* didn't see any problem—or at least appeared not to. A convenient fog.

Murdoch came up with a tactic to try to lift the fog. Instead of just lowering his price back down to 40 cents, he announced his intention to lower it to 25 cents. The people at the *Daily News* doubted that Murdoch could afford to pull it off. Moreover, they believed that their recent success was due to a superior product and not just to the dime price advantage. They were not particularly threatened by Murdoch's announcement.

Seeing no response, Murdoch tried a second tactic. He started the price reduction on Staten Island as a test run. As a result, sales of the *Post* doubled– and the fog lifted. The *Daily News* learned that its readers were remarkably willing to read the *Post* in order to save 15 cents. The paper's added value was not so large after all. Suddenly, it didn't seem so stupid for Murdoch to have lowered his price to a quarter. It became clear that disastrous consequences would befall the *Daily News* if Murdoch extended his price cut throughout New York City. In London, just such a meltdown scenario was taking place between Murdoch's *Times* and Conrad Black's *Daily Telegraph*. It was in the context of all these events that the *Daily News* raised its price to 50 cents.

Only the *New York Times* remained in a fog. Murdoch had never wanted to lower his price to 25 cents. He never would have expected the *Daily News* to stay at 40 cents had he initiated an across-the-board cut to 25 cents. Murdoch's announcement and the test run on Staten Island were simply tactics designed to get the *Daily News* to raise its price. With price parity, the *Post* no longer would be losing subscribers, and both papers would be more profitable than if they were priced at 25 cents or even at 40 cents. Coopetition strikes again. The *Post* took an initial hit in raising its price to 50 cents, and when the *Daily News* tried to be greedy and not follow suit, Murdoch showed it the light. When the *Daily News* raised its price, it was not daring Murdoch at all. It was saving itself–and Murdoch–from a price war.

In the case of the *Daily News* and the *Post*, the fog was convenient to the former but not to the latter. So Murdoch lifted it.

Disagreeing to Agree

Sometimes, a fog is convenient to all parties. A fee negotiation between an investment bank and its client (a composite of several confidential negotiations) offers a good example. The client is a company whose owners are forced to sell. The investment bank has identified a potential acquirer. So far, the investment bank has been working on good faith, and now it's time to sign a fee letter.

The investment bank suggests a 1% fee. The client figures that its company will fetch

$500 million and argues that a $5 million
fee would be excessive. It proposes a
0.625% fee. The investment bankers think
that the price will be closer to $250 million
and that accepting the client's proposal
would cut their expected fee from $2.5
million to about $1.5 million.

One tactic would be to lift the fog. The
investment bank could try to convince the
client that a $500 million valuation is unre-
alistic and that its fear of a $5 million fee is
therefore unfounded. The problem with this
tactic is that the client does not want to hear
a low valuation. Faced with such a prospect,
it might walk away from the deal and even
from the bank altogether—and then there
would be no fee.

The client's optimism and the investment bankers' pessimism create an opportunity for an agreement rather than an argument. Both sides should agree to a 0.625% fee combined with a $2.5 million guarantee. That way, the client gets the percentage it wants and considers the guarantee a throw-away. With a 0.625% fee, the guarantee kicks in only for a sales price below $400 million, and the client expects the price to be $100 million higher. Because the investment bankers expected $2.5 million under their original proposal, now that this fee is guar-anteed, they can agree to a lower percentage.

Negotiating over pure percentage fees is inherently win-lose. If the fee falls from 1% to 0.625%, the client wins and the investment bankers lose. Going from 1% to 0.625% plus a floor is win-win—but only when the two parties maintain different perceptions. The fog allows for coopetition.

CHANGING THE SCOPE

After players, added values, rules, and tactical possibilities, there is nothing left to change within the existing boundaries of the game. But no game is an island. Games are linked across space and over time. A game in one place can affect games elsewhere, and a game today can influence games tomorrow. You can change the scope of a game. You can expand it by creating linkages to other games, or you can shrink it by severing linkages. Either approach may work to your benefit.

We left Nintendo with a stock market value exceeding both Sony's and Nissan's, and with Mario better known than Mickey Mouse. Sega and other would-be rivals had failed in the 8-bit game. But while the rest fell by the wayside, Sega didn't give up. It introduced a new 16-bit system to the U.S. market. It took two years before Nintendo responded with its own 16-bit machine. By then, with the help of its game hero, Sonic the Hedgehog, Sega had established a secure and significant market position. Today the two companies roughly split the 16-bit market.

Was Sega lucky to get such a long, uncontested period in which to establish itself?

Did Nintendo simply blow it? We think not. Nintendo's 8-bit franchise was still very valuable. Sega realized that by expanding the scope, it could turn Nintendo's 8-bit strength into a 16-bit weakness. Put yourself in Nintendo's shoes: Would you jump into the 16-bit game or hold back? Had Nintendo jumped into the game, it would have meant competition and, hence, lower 16-bit prices. Lower prices for 16-bit games, substitutes for 8-bit games, would have reduced the value created by the 8-bit games–a big hit to Nintendo's bottom line. Letting Sega have the 16-bit market all to itself meant that 16-bit prices were higher than they otherwise would have been. Higher 16-bit prices cushioned the effect of the new-generation technology on the old. By staying out of Sega's way, Nintendo made a calculated trade-off: Give up a piece of the 16-bit action in order to extend the life of the 8-bit market. Nintendo's decision to hold back was reasonable, given the link between 8-bit and 16-bit games. Note that the decision not to create competition in a substitutes market is the mirror image of 3DO's strategy of creating competition in a complements market.

THE TRAPS OF STRATEGY

Changing the game is hard. There are many potential traps. Our mind-set, map, and method for changing the game–coopetition, the Value Net, and PARTS–are designed to help managers recognize and avoid these traps.

The first mental trap is to think you have to accept the game you find yourself in. Just realizing that you can change the game is crucial. There's more work to be done, but it's far more rewarding to be a game maker than a game taker.

The next trap is to think that changing the game must come at the expense of others. Such thinking can lead to an embattled mind-set that causes you to miss win-win opportunities. The coopetition mind-set—looking for both win-win and win-lose strategies—is far more rewarding.

Another trap is to believe that you have to find something to do that others can't. When you do come up with a way to change the game, accept that your actions might well be imitated. Being unique is not a prerequisite for success. Imitation can be healthy, as the GM card story and others illustrate.

The fourth trap is failing to see the whole game. What you don't see, you can't change. In particular, many people overlook the role of complementors. The solution is to draw the Value Net for your business; it will double your repertoire of strategies for changing the game. Any strategy toward customers has a counterpart with suppliers (and vice versa), and any strategy with substitutors has a mirror image for complementors (and vice versa).

The fifth trap is failing to think methodically about changing the game. Using

PARTS as a comprehensive, theory-based set of levers helps generate strategies, but that is not enough. To understand the effect of any particular strategy, you need to go beyond your own perspective. Be allocentric, not egocentric.

For the Holland Sweetener Company, it would have helped to recognize that Coke and Pepsi would have paid a high price up front to make the aspartame market competitive. BellSouth succeeded with a weak hand only because it understood the incentives of Lin and McCaw. Nintendo's power in the 8-bit game came from lowering everyone else's added value. To craft the right choice of capacity and price, Kiwi had to put itself in the shoes of the major airlines to ensure that they would have a greater incentive to accommodate rather than fight Kiwi's entry. The effect of a meet-the-competition clause becomes clear only after you consider how a challenger thinks you would respond to an attempt it might make to steal one of your customers. To achieve his ends, Murdoch had to recognize that the *Daily News* was in a fog and find a way to lift it. By understanding how different parties perceive the game differently, a negotiator is better able to forge an agreement. Sega's success depended on the dilemma it created for Nintendo by starting a new 16-bit game linked to the existing 8-bit game.

Finally, there is no silver bullet for changing the game of business. It is an ongoing process. Others will be trying to change the game, too. Sometimes their changes will work to your benefit and sometimes not. You may need to change the game again. There is, after all, no end to the game of changing the game.

NOTES

The authors are grateful to F. William Barnett, Putnam Coes, Amy Guggenheim, Michael Maples, Anna Minto, Troy Paredes, Harborne Stuart, Bart Troyer, Michael Tuchen, and Peter Wetenhall, along with many other colleagues and students, for their generous comments and suggestions.

    1. In-depth discussion and applications of the principle of looking forward and reasoning backward are provided in *Thinking Strategically: The Competitive Edge in Business, Politics, and Everyday Life*, by

Avinash Dixit and Barry Nalebuff (W.W. Norton, 1991).

2. The argument is spelled out in Adam Brandenburger and Harborne Stuart, "Value-based Business Strategy," which will appear in a forthcoming issue of *Journal of Economics & Management Strategy*.

3. This portmanteau word can be traced to Ray Noorda, CEO of Novell, who has used it to describe relationships in the information technology business: "You have to cooperate and compete at the same time" (*Electronic Business Buyer*, December 1993).

4. McCaw paid $26.5 million to Los Angeles RCC—a joint venture between McCaw and BellSouth that was 85% owned by BellSouth. Since McCaw did not get any additional equity for his investment, it was in essence a $22.5 million payment to BellSouth and a $4 million payment to himself. Security laws override antitrust laws, so it's legal for one bidder to pay another not to be a player.

5. Unfortunately, the program provided little comfort to Cozzi, who resigned when TWA scaled it

back. TWA returned to full-scale Comfort Class in the fall of 1994.

6. On a separate issue, Nintendo made a settlement with the Federal Trade Commission in which it agreed to stop requiring retailers to adhere to a minimum price for the game console. Further, Nintendo would give previous buyers a $5-off coupon toward future purchases of Nintendo game cartridges. Reflecting on the case, *Barron's* suggested that "the legion of trust-busting lawyers would be far more productively occupied playing Super Mario Brothers 3 than bringing cases of this kind" (December 3, 1991).

ABOUT THESE AUTHORS

Adam M. Brandenburger is the J.P. Valles Professor of Business Economics and Strategy at the Stern School of Business at New York University in New York.

Barry J. Nalebuff is the Milton Steinbach professor at Yale School of Management in New Haven, Connecticut.

The authors' research, teaching, and consulting focus on game theory and business strategy.

ALSO BY THESE AUTHORS

Harvard Business Review Articles

"Inside Intel"

* 9 7 8 1 6 3 3 6 9 5 2 7 6 *